MAN-MADE MARVELS!

GUINNESS WORLD RECORDS

by **DONALD LEMKE**

An Imprint of HarperCollinsPublishers

GUINNESS WORLD RECORDS: OFFICIALLY AMAZING

Since 1955, Guinness World Records has been the world's most trusted, accurate, and recognized source for record-breaking achievements. From the tallest building to the fastest fire truck to the largest electric guitar, Guinness World Records is home to the most outrageous marvels of engineering, including the Officially Amazing feats in this book!

Guinness World Records holders are truly amazing, but all attempts to set or break records are performed under controlled conditions and at the participant's own risk. Please seek out the appropriate guidance before you attempt any record-breaking activities.

Guinness World Records: Man-Made Marvels!
© 2016 Guinness World Records Limited.
The words GUINNESS WORLD RECORDS and related
logos are trademarks of Guinness World Records Limited.
Image of Tallest Residential Building (page 9) © Alamy
All records and information accurate as of November 2015.
All rights reserved. Printed in the United States of America.
No part of this book may be used or reproduced in any manner
whatsoever without written permission except in the case of brief
quotations embodied in critical articles and reviews. For information
address HarperCollins Children's Books, a division of HarperCollins
Publishers, 195 Broadway, New York, NY 10007.
www.harpercollinschildrens.com

Library of Congress Control Number: 2016936057
ISBN 978-0-06-234180-8

Design by Erica De Chavez and Eugene Vosough
16 17 18 19 20   PC/RRDC   10 9 8 7 6 5 4 3 2 1
❖
First Edition

SECTION ONE:

ARCHITECTURE & SCULPTURE

Guinness World Records is home to fascinating, immense, and breathtaking feats of engineering. In this section, discover awe-inspiring architecture and awesome human-made sculptures—from the world's tallest buildings to the longest bridges and supersize statues. Prepare to be amazed.

The world's **tallest building**, the Burj Khalifa Tower, stands 2,716 feet, 6 inches above Dubai, United Arab Emirates (UAE), casting a monstrous shadow across this desert city. Completed on December 30, 2009, this breathtaking building has been an impressive example of architectural engineering ever since.

Serving guests in the Burj Khalifa is a mighty tall order—the *tallest*, in fact! Thankfully, the world's **tallest building** is also home to the **highest restaurant from ground level**. From Level 122 of the tower, patrons at Atmosphere enjoy a view of Dubai from 1,447 feet above the city. Order up . . . *way* up!

A real-life bridge over troubled waters . . . the Akashi Kaikyō Bridge, also known as the Pearl Bridge, is the **longest cable suspension bridge**, with a main span of 6,532 feet, or 1.24 miles. This engineering marvel links Honshu and Shikoku, Japan, across the Akashi Strait, an area known for some of the worst storms on Earth and some of the deadliest waters. Engineers designed the structure to withstand winds of 180 miles per hour (mph).

From the Gold Rush to rush hour, San Francisco, California, has a long—and *wide*—history! On September 2, 2013, the east span of the San Francisco–Oakland Bay Bridge opened, making it the world's **widest bridge**. The bridge features a total deck width of 258 feet. Its 10 lanes of roadway support approximately 270,000 horn-honking vehicles every day.

BOLD BRIDGE-MAKING

The Newport Transporter Bridge, which spans the River Usk in Wales, UK, stretches 594 feet, making it the **longest transporter bridge**. Constructed in 1906, the bridge still forms part of the British public road network, ferrying vehicles across the river on a gondola suspended by cables from an overhead track. It was designed by French engineer Ferdinand Arnodin.

The San Francisco–Oakland Bay Bridge opened in 1936 but was left crippled by the Loma Prieta earthquake in 1989. In 2002, restoration and replacement work began on the bridge at an estimated cost of $6.3 billion, making it not just the **widest** but also the **most expensive bridge**.

First built in 1867, the Hōrai Bridge in Shizuoka Prefecture, Japan, holds the Guinness World Records title for the **longest wooden footbridge**. It measures 2,944 feet and would take, on average, nearly 1,200 steps to cross!

The Kokonoe Yume Bridge in Kokonoe, Japan, holds the record for the **longest suspension bridge for pedestrians**, spanning a length of 1,279 feet. In Japanese, the word *yume* means "dream." But with its narrow, 5-foot-wide walkway, crossing this bridge might feel more like a nightmare if you're afraid of heights!

Ever dream of sleeping on a cloud? At JW Marriott Marquis in Dubai, UAE, formerly known as Emirates Park Towers Hotel & Spa, guests can sleep *above* them! As the world's **tallest hotel**, JW Marriott Marquis's 77-floor twin towers stand 1,165 feet, 10 inches tall and feature 1,368 luxury rooms and 240 suites.

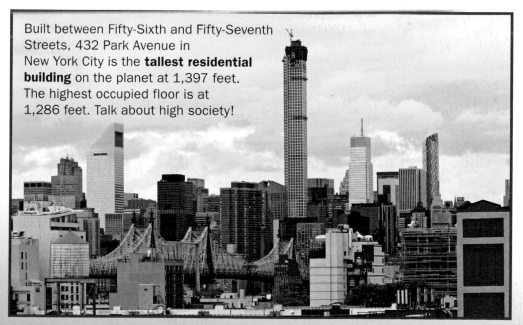

Built between Fifty-Sixth and Fifty-Seventh Streets, 432 Park Avenue in New York City is the **tallest residential building** on the planet at 1,397 feet. The highest occupied floor is at 1,286 feet. Talk about high society!

They sure don't build 'em like they used to! Constructed in 1912, the Woolloomooloo Bay Wharf in Sydney, Australia, remains the **largest wooden building**. The structure stretches 1,312 feet long, 206 feet wide, and stands five stories tall. The building houses residents and retail spaces—and hopefully no termites!

It can take as much engineering skill to get rid of a massive building as it takes to build one. The **largest structure demolished** to date was the Kingdome arena in Seattle, Washington, with an interior volume of 19.8 million cubic feet. A staggering 4,700 pounds of explosives had to be used to take it down.

How do you move a 29,080-ton building? On wheels, of course . . . and very, very carefully! In 1999, the Shubert Theatre in Minneapolis, Minnesota, became the **largest building relocated on wheels**. It took Artspace Projects, Inc. 13 days, from February 9 through 21, to move the massive building just three blocks.

When you want to move a 33.3-million-pound building in one piece, hire a professional! In November 2004, the Guangzhou Luban Corporation set the world record by moving the Fu Gang Building at West Bank Road Wuzhou, in the Guangxi Province of China. It took 11 days to move the **heaviest building intact** approximately 117 feet.

BUILDING BREAKTHROUGHS

At the world's **smallest hotel**, the Eh'häusl in Amberg, Germany, three really is a crowd! At approximately 559 square feet, the hotel can accommodate only two guests at a time but does include a minispa!

Bettering his own record by 945 buildings, on November 17, 2015, Jon Lovitch of the USA constructed the **largest gingerbread village**, consisting of 1,102 sugary sweet buildings. The tasty town was displayed at the New York Hall of Science in Queens, New York.

In the world's **largest shopping center**, customers can literally shop till they drop! That's because the Dubai Mall, located in downtown Dubai, UAE, in the shadow of the Burj Khalifa (right), covers 12.1 million square feet! Opened in 2008, the massive mall contains 1,200 retail stores. It also contains 160 food and beverage outlets and even its very own dinosaur skeleton (inset below).

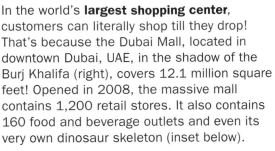

To truly experience the magnitude of space, you need a lot of, well, *space*! No planetarium boasts more of it than the one at the Nagoya City Science Museum in Japan. Suspended 37 feet above the ground, the almost perfectly spherical structure is 129 feet tall, making it the **largest planetarium** on planet Earth.

No aquarium can ever match a real sea in terms of scale, but Chimelong Ocean Kingdom in Guangdong, China, comes the closest! The **largest aquarium** has a total water volume of 12.87 million gallons (a combination of salt and fresh water). Part of a wider theme park, the watery attraction also boasts several other records, including **largest aquarium tank**—home to the **largest fish**, whale sharks—and **largest underwater viewing dome** (inset) with an external diameter of 39 feet, 4.4 inches.

Ladies and gentlemen, raise the roof for this next world record! The **longest roof covered by a metal corrugated sheet** is more than 659 feet. Showing off their mastery of metal, PT Utomodeck Metal Works constructed the record-breaking roof in Rembang City, Central Java, Indonesia, on September 1, 2013.

The Tokyo Skytree towers over all other towers on Earth! The world's **tallest tower**, formerly known as the New Tokyo Tower, rises 2,080 feet to the top of the mast in Japan's capital city. Completed in 2011, Tokyo Skytree is a broadcasting and observation tower that also features a sky-high restaurant, which is sure to serve upscale food.

FACT!

Want to know the difference between a tower and a building? It all comes down to usable floor space. Half of a building's height must be habitable, while a tower is 50 percent or less.

Air traffic controllers need their eyes on the sky, and they can't get them much closer than at Tower West at Kuala Lumpur International Airport 2 in Malaysia. Completed on April 30, 2013, the world's **tallest airport control tower** measures more than 438 feet tall.

HOW HIGH CAN THEY GO?

The Petronas Towers in Kuala Lumpur, Malaysia, hold the Guinness World Records title for **tallest matching pair of buildings**, each measuring 1,482 feet. The 88-story structures opened in March 1996.

On July 1, 2013, in Blanquefort, France, Camille Courgeon set a really sweet record. She built the **tallest sugar cube tower**, standing 6 feet, 10 inches. Courgeon completed the tower in just under 3 hours, using 2,669 sugar cubes.

Maintaining historic buildings requires history-making scaffolding. While repairing the New York City Municipal Building from 1988 to 1992, Regional Scaffolding & Hoisting Co., Inc. built the world's **tallest scaffolding tower**. Erecting the 650-foot structure required 20,000 aluminum planks and 12,000 scaffold frames. If stacked vertically, that's enough frames to rise 12 miles into the sky!

No one can predict when the next Guinness World Records title will fall . . . especially this one! The Church of Suurhusen in Germany holds the record for the **farthest leaning tower**, which leans with an angle of inclination of 5.1939 degrees. (By comparison, the Leaning Tower of Pisa in Italy is at approximately 3.99 degrees.) Here's hoping this record stands the test of time just a little longer.

The Oosterscheldedam, a storm-surge barrier in the southwest of the Netherlands, is the **largest tidal barrier**. It has 65 concrete piers and 62 steel gates and stretches a staggering 5.59 miles. Queen Beatrix of the Netherlands officially opened the dam on October 4, 1986.

The Grande Dixence Dam on the River Dixence in Switzerland is grand by name and grand by nature! The world's **highest concrete dam** was built between 1953 and 1961 to a height of 935 feet, with a crest length of 2,297 feet. Engineers used 210,400,000 cubic feet of concrete to complete the massive structure.

Not all dams are made of stone and concrete. The **longest rubber dam** measures 3,723 feet long and consists of 16 sections—each part is approximately 229 feet long. Completed on July 1, 1997, the Xiaobudong Dam is situated on the Yihe River in Shandong Province, China.

Six Flags Magic Mountain in Valencia, California, is riding high! As of May 2015, the resort had 19 operating roller coasters—the **most roller coasters in one theme park**. Many of these rides even boast individual records: for instance, Riddler's Revenge is the **fastest stand-up design roller coaster**, hitting an eye-watering 65 miles per hour, while X was the **first fourth-dimension roller coaster**, on which the seats are able to independently rotate 360 degrees!

The **steepest roller coaster** is located at the Fuji-Q Highland Amusement Park in Fujiyoshida City, Japan. Opening in 2011, Takabisha has an inclination of 121 degrees over 11 feet, 2 inches, and the ride's highest tower stands 141 feet off the ground. Descending from this peak, the coaster takes 0.38 seconds to complete its steepest stretch. That's faster than it takes to scream "AHHHHHHH!"

What goes up must come down . . . eventually! Full Throttle, a steel roller coaster also at Six Flags Magic Mountain in California, has the world's **tallest loop** at 127.13 feet. Now riding that has got to be a head rush!

COASTING INTO THE RECORD BOOKS

Colossos at Heide Park Soltau in Lower Saxony, Germany, is, well, colossal! It holds the Guinness World Records title for the **tallest wooden coaster** at 196 feet, 10 inches high.

The Steel Dragon 2000 at Nagashima Spa Land amusement park in Japan is any coaster enthusiast's fantasy. It holds the record as the **longest roller coaster**—twisting and turning for a staggering 1.54 miles.

Did you know Ferris wheels are sometimes called big wheels? This record-breaker certainly lives up to that extra-large nickname! Installed for the Puebla State Government, Mexico, in 2013, the R80 XL Ferris wheel made by Bussink Design of Switzerland is 100 percent mobile. With a diameter of 229 feet, this makes it the **largest transportable Ferris wheel**.

In Ashgabat, Turkmenistan, it's *fair* weather every day— even when it's raining outside! That's because the city is home to the world's **largest indoor Ferris wheel**, which opened on April 30, 2012. Standing more than 156 feet, 2 inches tall, this big-time ride is big-time fun—all year round!

George Washington Gale Ferris, Jr. unveiled the **first big wheel**, now named in his honor, at the 1893 World's Columbian Exposition in Chicago, Illinois. Ferris wheels have towered over fairs, carnivals, and amusement parks ever since, but none more than the Daikanransha big wheel (above) at Palette Town in Odaiba, Tokyo, Japan. As the world's **tallest big wheel**, this giant ride stands 394 feet tall and carries up to 384 passengers.

What's in a name? Riders aboard the **tallest swing carousel**, called Texas SkyScreamer, should know exactly what to expect. Towering 403 feet above Six Flags Over Texas in Arlington, Texas, the aptly named ride is sure to make anyone scream!

Cowabunga! At the world's **largest wave pool**, thrill seekers have plenty of room to hang 10 . . . or 20 . . . or 30! Located in Siam Park City, Bangkok, Thailand, the pool covers more than 146,388 square feet. It's no wonder that it's often called an artificial sea.

The **largest inflatable castle** is fit for a king, a queen . . . and a few hundred friends! The castle, designed by Dana Caspersen and William Forsythe and constructed by Southern Inflatables (all from the UK), stood 39 feet tall and was 62 feet square at the base. Between March 24 and May 11, 1997, visitors to the Roundhouse in Camden, London, UK, got the royal tour of this bouncy fortress.

How do you climb the **tallest indoor ice climbing wall**? *Brrr*-footed! Opened on November 19, 2005, in Seoul, South Korea, visitors to the O_2 World can ascend this record-breaking ice wall, which measures more than 65 feet tall and 42 feet wide—if they don't get cold feet, of course!

Most malls play elevator music, but the Lotte Department Store in Busan, South Korea, plays "water music" owing to being home to the **tallest indoor music fountain.** The water feature can shoot its jets nearly 60 feet high!

If Old Man Winter needed a place to crash, he'd probably choose the ICEHOTEL—the **largest ice structure**—in Sweden, which is rebuilt every year after melting in the spring. In December 2002, a total of 700 people were housed in 140 igloos at the site for the employees of food packaging company Tetra Pak, also earning it the record for **largest ice village** (above).

Guinness World Records titles don't grow on trees, but some are grown on buildings! Eco-friendly companies Cleanaway and Shine Green Energy from Chinese Taipei created a 27,919-square-foot green wall—the **largest vertical garden**—to conceal a landfill site, as verified on June 29, 2015.

On February 26, 2008, residents of Bethel, Maine, and surrounding towns, completed the world's **tallest snow woman**—122 feet, 1 inch tall. The record-breaking sculpture, nicknamed Olympia, has long since melted, but who knows? Maybe, like Frosty, she'll be back again someday!

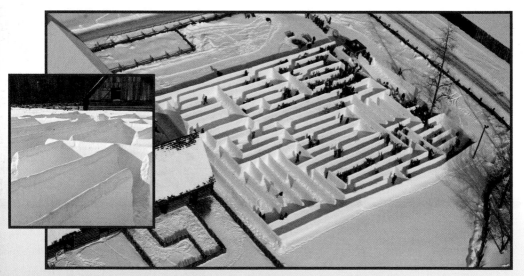

On February 15, 2015, the Fort William Historical Park in Thunder Bay, Canada, created the **largest snow maze**—covering more than 18,255 square feet—as part of the annual Voyageur Winter Carnival.

Talk about a-MAZE-ing engineering feats! The **largest ice maze** was laid out like a buffalo and spanned more than 12,855 square feet. It was sponsored by Arctic Glacier at the Powder Keg festival in Buffalo, New York, on February 26, 2010.

PATHS TO WORLD RECORDS

The **largest vertical maze** is situated on the front facade of Al Rostamani Maze Tower in Dubai, UAE, and has a surface area in excess of 42,487 square feet.

The **largest permanent hedge maze** is the Pineapple Garden Maze at the Dole Plantation in Wahiawa, Hawaii, which spans 3.15 acres. It also holds the record for the **longest path in a permanent hedge maze**, with 2.46 miles of winding path.

If you're lost in the woods, like the fabled Hansel and Gretel, the **largest gingerbread house** would be easy to spot! Created on November 30, 2013, by Traditions Club in Bryan, Texas, the delicious dwelling had an internal volume of 39,201.8 cubic feet. That's enough gingerbread to satisfy any sweet tooth!

Do you happen to have 50,342 K'NEX blocks lying around? Then you could re-create the world's **largest K'NEX tower**! From June 5 to 6, 1999, K'NEX Manufacturing built a toy tower measuring more than 101 feet tall, setting a new Guinness World Records title.

How do you build a Guinness World Records–worthy structure? Brick by brick. On May 18, 1996, in Taipei City, Taiwan, a team of 800 people completed the **tallest toy brick pyramid** to commemorate the inauguration of Taiwanese President Lee Teng-hui. The structure measured a staggering 82 feet, 2 inches high.

The world record for the **largest K'NEX sculpture** belongs to the BLOODHOUND SSC RBLI K'NEX Build Team in London, UK. Their record-breaking replica of the famous car that is aiming to break the 1,000-mile-per-hour barrier measured 43 feet, 10.7 inches long and 8 feet wide. Hopefully the real Bloodhound SSC will set its own record one day soon!

Can't imagine a life without LEGO®? How about a life *inside* LEGO? On September 17, 2009, British TV presenter James May and 1,200 volunteers for *James May's Toy Stories* built the **largest life-size LEGO house** in Dorking, UK. The structure was 15 feet, 4 inches high; 30 feet, 9 inches long; and 18 feet, 10 inches wide, with two floors and four rooms.

Nothing can top the world's **largest LEGO house**, right? Well, how about the world's **tallest LEGO tower**? Completed on June 21, 2015, the tallest structure built with interlocking plastic bricks measured 114 feet, 11 inches. Organized by LEGO Italia in Milan, Italy, the tower comprised an estimated 550,000 bricks and was contributed to by some 18,000 builders over four days.

Created by visitors of the SteinZeit im phaeno exhibition in Wolfsburg, Germany, on October 6, 2008, the **longest span of a bridge made from LEGO bricks** stretched an incredible 45 feet, 11 inches. That's about the same length as four great white sharks in a row!

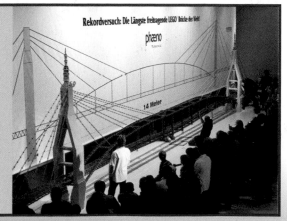

All aboard! (And we do mean *all*.) The Wilmington Railroad Museum Model Railroad Committee achieved the Guinness World Records title for the **longest model train**. Presented in Wilmington, North Carolina, on April 23, 2011, the train measured 925 feet, 6 inches long and was made up of 31 locomotives and 1,563 carriages.

They thought they could . . . they thought they could . . . and they did! On May 11, 2013, TOMY assembled the world's **tallest continuous toy train track** at Grand Central Terminal in New York City. The track measured 17 feet, 4 inches from the ground to the highest point.

MORE TREMENDOUS TRAINS

The **highest average speed by a train over a distance of 1,000 kilometers** (621 miles) is 190.37 mph. The record was set by an SNCF TGV train, between Calais and Marseille in France, on May 26, 2001.

The Guinness World Records title for the **longest passenger train** belongs to the National Belgian Railway Company. The train measured 5,685 feet and consisted of 70 coaches pulled by just one electric locomotive.

If you've ever dreamed of flying like Superman, skydiving wind tunnels offer a surprisingly similar experience. On August 6, 2013, Inflight Dubai achieved the record for the **largest indoor skydiving wind tunnel**, with an internal volume of 14,858.12 cubic feet. That's more than enough room to spread your wings and fly!

Breaking a world record can make someone a star, but sometimes it's the other way around! The **largest architectural star** is a 34,875-square-foot glass-clad octagonal structure at the base of a television tower in Ashgabat, Turkmenistan. The supersize star was unveiled during an opening ceremony on October 17, 2011.

American Dale Gasteier holds the record for the **largest freestanding illuminated star**. He built the 52-foot-long star structure, which stands 76 feet tall on its support tower, to celebrate Thanksgiving in 1998. One thousand lights illuminate the star during the holiday season and it is visible from up to four miles away.

Even on the darkest night, a lantern can light your way . . . or even the whole sky! On March 10, 2008, the Nenbutsushu Sanpouzan Muryojuji Temple in Kato City, Hyogo, Japan, achieved the **largest stone lantern**: 39 feet, 4 inches tall and 24 feet, 3 inches wide.

You won't be taking the **tallest lantern** on any camping trips—unless you're Paul Bunyan! On March 30, 2012, the organizing committee for the first Wuhan-Chengdu International Giant Panda Lantern Show in Wuhan City, Hubei, China, created the record-setting light. It measured a colossal 69 feet, 4.67 inches tall.

Tyler
Texas

Ever try stacking one golf ball on top of another? It might seem impossible to most, but not for Cal Shipman and the First Tee of Greater Tyler at Mamie G. Griffin Elementary School in Tyler, Texas. On January 31, 2014, they stacked 16,206 golf balls without adhesive to complete the **largest ball pyramid**.

Christmas pyramids are traditional German holiday decorations. Often depicting nativity scenes, these tiered wooden structures typically stand only a few inches to a few feet high. But the world's **tallest Christmas pyramid** is anything but typical! Created by German Henry Jacob, the record-breaking decoration towered 65 feet, 7 inches above the Berlin Christmas Market in 2010.

Ever dreamed of a 3,100-scoop ice-cream cone? Well, that's the exact number of scoops Baskin-Robbins International used to construct the **largest ice-cream scoop pyramid** on May 18, 2000, in Maui, Hawaii. That would give even the biggest ice-cream fan mega brain freeze!

On November 20, 2012, in São Paulo, Brazil, Ivan Zarif Neto, Rafael Migani Monteiro, and Fernando Gama jointly achieved the record for the **tallest toilet-paper roll pyramid**— 13 feet, 5 inches tall. The pyramid was comprised of 23,821 separate rolls!

When others say you can't, just say you *can*! Transmed Overseas and Pringles (both from the UAE) proved they *could* on November 12, 2015, when they stacked a mind-boggling 31,001 cans of Pringles chips to make the **largest can pyramid** in Dubai, UAE.

Recycling is the act of creating something new from items that have been used before. On April 25, 2015, Indian Pinak Naik piled 85,853 old LED light boxes to create the **largest cardboard box pyramid** at the Kumar Pacific Mall in Pune, India. Now that's recycling on a record-breaking scale!

These record-breakers deserve a coffee break! On October 8, 2010, Melanie Lütkenfent, Vanessa Höft, Miriam Plümer, Arman Schlieker, and Damian Krey (all from Germany), in association with Aral AG, constructed the **largest coffee cup pyramid**. Standing 13 feet, 7 inches tall, the pyramid consisted of 22,140 cups!

MORE PRESTIGIOUS PYRAMIDS

The pyramid of Khufu at Giza, Egypt, also known as the Great Pyramid, is the world's **tallest pyramid**. It likely measured more than 481 feet high when completed around 4,500 years ago. Erosion and vandalism have reduced its height to 451 feet high today.

Money can't buy a Guinness World Records title, but you can build one with it! The **largest coin pyramid** consisted of 723,456 coins and was achieved by "THE" Million Cents at the DCT Education Park in Hong Kong, China, on December 3, 2013.

Superheroes aren't the only ones who can bend steel. Sculptors can, too! On May 23, 2014, in Incheon, South Korea, artist Ohin Kwon achieved the record for the **largest steel sculpture**: it stands more than 77 feet tall and depicts a fortune bear—a figure from Korean mythology.

This record really *rocks*! The statue of the God of Longevity is the **largest stone carving** in the world. Located on the northwest side of the Guimeng peak in the Meng Shan Mountains near Pingyi, China, the sculpture measures 656 feet wide and 715 feet high.

REAL GEMS

Weighing 545.67 carats, the Golden Jubilee Diamond is the **largest cut diamond**. The giant gem was purchased from diamond trader De Beers by a Thai business syndicate and presented to the king of Thailand to commemorate his golden jubilee in 1996. It is now mounted in the Thai royal scepter.

The **largest carved sapphire** is a multicolored polished rock that weighs 80,500 carats. The giant gemstone was displayed during the annual Unifour Gem & Mineral & Jewelry Show at the Hickory Metro Convention, North Carolina, on March 19, 2005.

On August 19, 2008, in Porrentruy, Switzerland, Michel Schmid completed the world's **largest wooden sculpture**. Depicting a Sioux head, the wooden wonder measures 75 feet, 2 inches tall.

The next time that you're eating breakfast, just think about all the construction possibilities in front of you! On March 14, 2014, in Shanghai, China, Zoe Shanghai Co. Ltd. built the **largest toast structure**. It measured 7 feet, 3 inches long; 4 feet, 6 inches wide; and 7 feet, 2.61 inches tall. We'll raise a toast to that!

On September 21, 2013, at Toyohashi Park in Aichi, Japan, Junior Chamber International Toyohashi built the **largest aluminum-can sculpture**. It used 104,840 cans and re-created a traditional Japanese castle.

The story behind this Guinness World Records title is actually 649,000 stories. . . . That's the total number of books used by Uruguayan artist Luz Darriba to construct the **largest book structure**, which she installed around the city walls of Lugo, Spain, and unveiled on November 30, 2000. That's one way of making it into the record books!

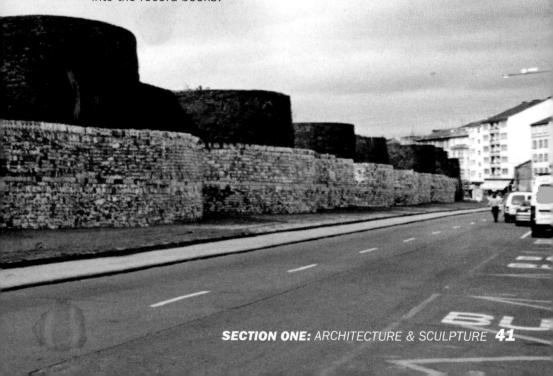

Artist Gintaras Karosas has a lot of TVs, but he's no couch potato! He created the world's **largest television sculpture** at the Open-Air Museum in Vilnius, Lithuania. Entitled *LNK Infotree*, the sculpture was made from 2,903 individual TV sets, over an area of 33,744.85 square feet.

David Reynolds of the UK is unmatched in his record. In July 2009, he completed the **largest matchstick model**. Titled *Cathedrals of the Sea*, the model consists of 4.075 million matchsticks and depicts a North Sea oil rig.

Not to be picky, but the **largest display of toothpick sculptures** consists of 101—*not* 100—sculptures! Stan Munro created the display at the Phelps Arts Center in Phelps, New York, on May 15, 2014. Munro is no one-*pick* pony, either. In 2013, he built a 16-foot, 8.4-inch replica of the world's **tallest building**, the Burj Khalifa—earning him the title for the **tallest toothpick sculpture**, too.

The **smallest handmade sculpture** is of a motorbike called *Golden Journey*, and was created by artist Willard Wigan, MBE of Birmingham, UK. The completely gold sculpture is 0.0063 inches long and sits inside a hollowed-out section of a single strand of beard stubble!

SECTION ONE: *ARCHITECTURE & SCULPTURE* **43**

Whoa, Christmas tree! The **largest plastic bottle sculpture**, standing 52 feet tall and representing a giant Christmas tree, was created by Jolanta Smidtiene in Kaunas, Lithuania. The festive sculpture contained 42,000 bottles in 2011!

In 2012, master chocolatier Andrew Farrugia of Malta created a beautiful, lifelike train using only chocolate. Stretching 111 feet, 8 inches long, the tasty work of art displayed at a railway station in Belgium was the **longest chocolate sculpture**.

Guinness World Records holders have *big* dreams. Catching those dreams can be tricky, unless you have a supersize dream catcher over your bed! Originating in Native American Ojibwe culture, dream catchers are said to capture bad dreams and only let good ones pass through. The **largest dream catcher** measures 9 feet, 10 inches in diameter and 31 feet, 7 inches in circumference. It was created by Frooviow TV, House PR, and Sketchevents (all from the UK) in 2012.

On August 29, 2009, 800 people of the Peace Piece Project at the Hiroshima Shudo University in Japan entered the Guinness World Records family by constructing the **largest origami crane**. The house-size paper bird had a wingspan of 268 feet, 9 inches. In Japanese legend, it is said that anyone who folds a thousand paper cranes will be granted a wish by a real crane.

The world's **tallest commemorative monument** is the stainless steel Gateway Arch in St. Louis, Missouri. Completed on October 28, 1965, to commemorate the westward expansion after the Louisiana Purchase of 1803, the arch spans 630 feet and rises to the same height. Finnish-American architect Eero Saarinen designed the structure, which cost an estimated $29 million to build.

Native peoples of the Arctic region of North America, including Inuit, Yupik, and others, once built stone sculptures called *inukshuks* to mark travel routes, hunting areas, and other destinations. Jose Melo of Allstone Quarry Products Inc. used some 180,000 pounds of granite to make the **tallest *inukshuk*—** 37 feet, 3.9 inches—in Schomberg, Ontario, Canada, on September 13, 2007.

The **largest Hindu temple** is the Swaminarayan Akshardham, built by BAPS Swaminarayan Sanstha in New Delhi, India. Opened on November 6, 2005, the towering temple is made entirely from pink sandstone and Italian marble and covers a total area of 86,342 square feet. It also contains 148 life-size elephant statues!

Some might long for a dinner reservation at Bellini, but others might have reservations about dining there. That's because it holds the record for the **largest revolving restaurant**! Located on the 45th floor of Mexico City's World Trade Center, the dizzying dining room has a floor area of 11,244.58 square feet.

Another *whirled* record coming up! The **largest revolving stage** measured 32 feet, 10 inches by 31 feet and was used by Hong Kong musician and dancer Aaron Kwok for a live concert at the AsiaWorld Arena in Hong Kong, China, on February 17, 2008.

This Guinness World Records feat might seem like a card trick, but it's not! On October 16, 2007, in Dallas, Texas, American Bryan Berg built the **tallest house of cards**, which soared to 25 feet, 9 inches high.

Bryan Berg should really be called the King of Cards! On March 10, 2010, he also achieved the **largest playing card structure**, a replica of the Venetian Macao resort in Macau, China. Comprised of 4,000 decks of cards, the final model measured 34 feet, 1.05 inches long and 9 feet, 5.39 inches tall. It took 44 days to complete.

The legendary Fountain of Youth may have been found at the Jean Philippe Pâtisserie in Bellagio Hotel and Casino, Las Vegas, Nevada. That's where the **tallest chocolate fountain** is located. The confectionary feature measures 26 feet, 3 inches tall and circulates 4,409 pounds of chocolate at a rate of 120 quarts per minute—enough chocolate to make anyone feel young again!

The Girl Scouts of Nassau County proved that cookies don't always crumble—sometimes they break . . . records, that is! On January 9, 2010, the group achieved the title for the **tallest cookie tower**—6 feet, 1 inch, using 22,800 cookies at the Roosevelt Field Mall in Garden City, New York.

SUCH SWEET FEATS

On February 10, 2012, in Osaka, Japan, Namba Walk created the **largest chocolate candy sculpture**. The marble chocolate heart covered in multicolored sugar sprinkles weighed 589 pounds, 8 ounces, and measured 5 feet, 0.5 inches long.

On September 28, 2014, in Zurich, Switzerland, the Jacobs Foundation, in collaboration with CARMA/Barry Callebaut Schweiz AG, achieved the **longest chocolate candy sculpture**—stretching 82 feet, 9 inches.

This record holder has a step up on the competition—11,674 steps, to be exact! That's the number of steps on the **longest stairway**, created for the Niesenbahn funicular railway near Spiez, Switzerland. The service stairs top out at a dizzying height of 5,476 feet.

This engineering feat walked its way straight into the record books. The **longest wooden walkway** is located in Dalian, China, and is 13.04 miles in length. Dalian Landscape & Garden Administration completed the walkway on August 28, 2009. The city is known for its many parks, rocky beaches, and rolling green mountains.

SECTION TWO:

VEHICLES & TRANSPORTATION

While some man-made marvels stand the test of time, others are always on the move! In this section, learn about record-breaking modes of transportation, from the world's smallest vehicles to the fastest and the largest. Buckle up for these remarkable rides!

Zbigniew Rózanek of Poland holds the Guinness World Records title for the **smallest bicycle**, with a 0.43-inch-diameter front wheel and a 0.51-inch rear wheel. On August 11, 1999, he rode the itty-bitty bike for a distance of 16 feet. There's no word on whether or not he popped the world's teeniest wheelie, though!

This solar-powered vehicle really burns—rubber, that is! The record for the **fastest solar-powered car** is 56.75 mph, achieved by Kenjiro Shinozuka of Japan. He sped to glory driving Ashiya University's Sky Ace TIGA at Shimojishima Airport, in Okinawa, Japan, on August 20, 2014.

ソーラーカー世界最速記録挑戦
Fastest Solar-Powered Vehicle
スピード **91.333 km/h**

HERE COMES THE SUN
The *MS TÛRANOR PlanetSolar* (see right) is the record holder for the **largest solar-powered boat**, measuring more than 101 feet long, with a beam width of over 49 feet.

The Earth travels around the sun, but this solar-powered vehicle traveled around the Earth! By December 15, 2012, the Solar Car Project Hochschule Bochum of Germany had covered 18,487 miles—the **longest journey by a solar electric vehicle**. Heading west, the team departed from Adelaide, Australia, and finished in Mount Barker, Australia.

Why did the electric car break a record? It got a real *charge* out of it! The **greatest distance covered by an electric vehicle on a single charge** is just over 807 miles. Kenjiro Shinozuka, Kenta Itogi, Takao Takasaki, and Chieko Takasaki—all from Japan—achieved the feat at Ogata Solar Sports Line in Minamiakita, Japan, from November 13 to 15, 2013.

The next record holder proves that there's always something new under the sun! From April 26 to May 18, 2013, the *MS TÙRANOR PlanetSolar* of Switzerland and its crew of five achieved a new record for the **fastest transatlantic crossing by solar power**. They traveled from Las Palmas, Gran Canaria, in Spain, to Marigot, Saint Martin, in the Caribbean in just 22 days, 12 hours, and 32 minutes.

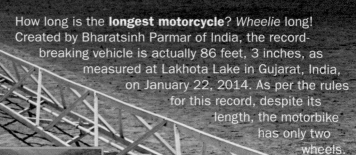

How long is the **longest motorcycle**? *Wheelie* long! Created by Bharatsinh Parmar of India, the record-breaking vehicle is actually 86 feet, 3 inches, as measured at Lakhota Lake in Gujarat, India, on January 22, 2014. As per the rules for this record, despite its length, the motorbike has only two wheels.

Italians Nicola Colombo and Valerio Fumagalli set the record for the **longest journey by electric motorcycle** during the Meneghina Express. They rode through 11 countries, starting in Shanghai, China, and ending in Milan, Italy, from June 10 to July 23, 2013, and covered a total distance of just over 7,691 miles.

This record-breaker is riding *high*! Italian Fabio Reggiani constructed the **tallest rideable motorcycle**. The big-time bike stands nearly 17 feet from the ground to the top of the handlebars and weighs in at more than 11,000 pounds.

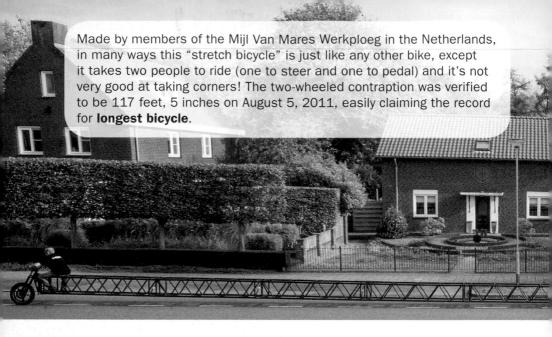

Made by members of the Mijl Van Mares Werkploeg in the Netherlands, in many ways this "stretch bicycle" is just like any other bike, except it takes two people to ride (one to steer and one to pedal) and it's not very good at taking corners! The two-wheeled contraption was verified to be 117 feet, 5 inches on August 5, 2011, easily claiming the record for **longest bicycle**.

This bike is the *wheel* deal! One of the world's best-known designers of unusual bikes, Didi Senft from Germany, built the **largest rideable bicycle**. When measured in 2012, in Pudagla, Germany, the bike stood just over 12 feet tall and each wheel was 10 feet, 9.92 inches across.

This record-breaking bike is souped-up . . . *way* up! American Richie Trimble is the proud owner of the **tallest rideable bicycle**, aptly named the Stoopidtall. It stands at 20 feet, 2.5 inches, as measured in Los Angeles, California, on December 26, 2013.

PEDAL POWER

The **most expensive bicycle sold at auction** went for $500,000 at Sotheby's in New York on November 1, 2009. Created by British artist Damien Hirst, the "Butterfly Bike" was ridden by Lance Armstrong during the final stage of the Tour de France in 2009.

Between August 1 and 30, 2014, American Troy Rank set a new record for the **longest journey on a motorized bicycle**—4,443.4 miles.

Most motorbikes are built light for speed, but not the Panzerbike! On November 23, 2007, in Zilly, Germany, Tilo and Wilfried Niebel of Harzer Bike Schmiede received the record for the **heaviest motorcycle**—10,470 pounds!

The **fastest speed reached on a conventional motorcycle by a female** is 232.522 mph, achieved by American Leslie Porterfield (pictured). She set the speed record on a modified Suzuki Hayabusa at Bonneville Salt Flats, Utah, on September 5, 2008. This is just behind the **fastest speed reached on a conventional motorcycle by a male**: also riding at Bonneville Salt Flats, in 2011, Richard Assen from New Zealand hit 261.315 mph.

Some people say good things come in small packages, and sometimes that includes Guinness World Records titles! In Hökerum, Sweden, in 2003, Tom Wilberg achieved the record for the **smallest motorcycle**. The micromachine has a front-wheel diameter of 0.62 inches, a rear-wheel diameter of 0.86 inches, a seat height of 2.55 inches, and a total weight of just 2 pounds, 6 ounces. To set this record, Wilberg rode the bike for more than 32 feet, reaching a top speed of 1.24 mph.

A monowheel has one wheel, but don't call it a unicycle! These speedy wheelers consist of one large wheel that revolves around a track, inside which the rider and engine are located. American Kerry McLean (pictured) first set the record for **fastest monowheel** in 2001, when he hit 57 mph. However, in 2015, the long-held record was overtaken by British racer Kevin Scott, who reached 61.18 mph riding the WarHorse monowheel at an airfield in Yorkshire, UK.

Bigger doesn't always mean better—sometimes it means best! In May 2010, in Arnhem, the Netherlands, Dutch engineer Wouter van den Bosch took a massive record-breaking ride on the **heaviest rideable tricycle**—his titan trike weighs 1,650 pounds.

Swiss carnival band Guggä Rugger Buus constructed a trike 26 feet, 7 inches long, achieving the record for the **longest tricycle**. Weighing 13,300 pounds, the three-wheeler served as a mobile grandstand for the 21 band members. That's one rockin' ride!

SECTION TWO: *VEHICLES & TRANSPORTATION* **65**

This outboard motor is out of this world! On a stretch of the Colorado River near Parker, Arizona, American Bob Wartinger set the record for the **fastest speed for an outboard motorboat**. He rocketed over the water at more than 176 mph on November 30, 1989.

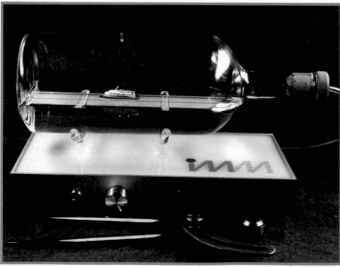

When it comes to Guinness World Records titles, even the smallest boats can make a big splash! In February 1998, the Institut für Mikrotechnik Mainz in Germany manufactured the **smallest motor-driven boat**. Powered by a single micromotor, the cute craft measured just 1.496 inches long, 0.472 inches wide, and 0.669 inches high.

Sometimes less is more, especially when it comes to fuel. New Zealanders Andrew Fenwick, Sam Fenwick, and Shaun Sutherland achieved the **greatest distance by an outboard motorboat on one gallon of fuel**. On July 1, 1999, at Orakei Basin, Auckland, New Zealand, they traveled 58.45 nautical miles on a trimaran-style skiff on that single gallon of gas.

Everyone knows that submarines operate underwater, but this one *tops* the competition! Canadian Pierre Poulin built the **smallest submarine** (left), with a displacement of 1,366 pounds, 14.4 ounces. Poulin piloted the sub, known as *BIG*, during a 43-minute dive in Memphremagog Lake, in Magog, Quebec, on June 26, 2005. In contrast, the **largest submarine** on record is the Russian 941 Akula class, aka *Typhoon*, which had a displacement of 58.4 million pounds!

MAKING WAVES

On October 13, 2013, at the Marina di Scilla, Italy, Giuseppe Cianti achieved the **fastest 100 meters** (328 feet) **in a pedal-powered boat** in 38.7 seconds.

The record for the **fastest propeller-driven boat** belongs to American Daryl Ehrlich. On November 22, 2009, at Firebird Raceway near Phoenix, Arizona, he attained 260.98 mph in his vessel, *Problem Child*.

Say "cheese"! In July 2008, researchers at the University of Delft in the Netherlands unveiled the DelFly Micro, the world's **smallest camera plane**. The dragonfly-shaped aerial drone weighs 0.105 ounces and has a wingspan of 4 inches. The pocket-size plane carries a tiny camera, which transmits live video to a controller on the ground.

The **smallest jet aircraft** is the home-built Bede BD-5J Microjet, owned by Juan Jimenez of San Juan, Puerto Rico. The aircraft weighs a mere 358 pounds and measures 12 feet long, with a wingspan of 17 feet. Despite its small size, the jet can hit 300 mph.

Markus Frey of Switzerland constructed the **largest model aircraft by wingspan**. On May 8, 2009, the plane, with wings 49 feet, 2 inches across, made its first flight at Buttwill Airfield in Switzerland.

SOUTHERN CROSS

Around the world in . . . 31 hours, 27 minutes, and 49 seconds! On August 15 to 16, 1995, Captains Michel Dupont and Claude Hetru achieved the **fastest circumnavigation by passenger aircraft** in an Air France Concorde. With 80 passengers and 18 crewmembers onboard, they flew from JFK Airport in New York eastbound via Toulouse, Dubai, Bangkok, Guam, Honolulu, and Acapulco, before landing back in New York.

Up, up, and *faraway*! The **farthest flight by an unmanned aircraft** is 8,600 miles, achieved by a USAF Northrop Grumman Global Hawk called *Southern Cross II*. The drone took off from Edwards Air Force Base in California on April 22, 2001, and landed at RAAF Base Edinburgh in South Australia nearly a day later.

Now here's a record worth writing home about. But Takuo Toda of Japan likely used all the paper he had handy to do so! On December 19, 2010, at the Fukuyama Big Rose Arena (pictured below), Toda launched the **longest flying paper aircraft**, which stayed aloft for 29.2 seconds. Of course, as the chairman of the Japan Airplane Origami Association, Toda has something of an advantage when it comes to folding paper planes. . . .

Nothing can stop this chopper! Australian Michael Farnan achieved the **farthest nonstop flight by a model helicopter over water** on May 23, 2001. Farnan piloted the radio-controlled aircraft from a real helicopter flying just behind for 62 miles, between Flinders Island and Deal Island, Australia, over the Bass Strait.

It is predicted that in the future, people will travel from place to place with their own personal aircraft. Well, the future is now! The world's **smallest helicopter** is the GEN H-4, made by the Gen Corporation of Japan. It has a rotor length of only 13 feet and weighs less than 155 pounds. Despite its size, this small whirlybird can transport a single passenger at speeds of 55 mph.

Some things are light as a feather, but how about light as a helicopter? Silverlit Toys Manufactory Ltd. holds the Guinness World Records title for the **lightest remote-controlled model helicopter**, the PicooZ MX-1. Manufactured in Causeway Bay, Hong Kong, the tiny toy aircraft weighs just 0.28 ounces—less than two pennies!

The record for the **largest airship in service** goes to the Zeppelin NT, manufactured by Zeppelin Luftschifftechnik of Germany. The airship stretches 246 feet and can carry 14 people. Despite weighing 2,500 pounds, the Zeppelin NT stays aloft simply on helium—the same gas that makes a birthday balloon float.

FLYING HIGH

In 2006, American Steve Fossett achieved the **longest nonstop flight** by any aircraft—26,389.3 miles—in the Virgin Atlantic GlobalFlyer. That's greater than the Earth's circumference through the Poles! The flight lasted an exhausting 76 hours, 45 minutes.

This Guinness World Records title holder deserves props—big props! The **largest airplane propeller** was the 22-foot, 6-inch–diameter Garuda propeller, fitted to a Linke-Hofmann R.II, which flew in 1919. Today, typical single-engine aircraft have propellers around 6 feet in diameter.

The **heaviest train carriage pulled by model trains** weighed 103,617 pounds. Two hundred Märklin BR 143 electric model locomotives, moving along 50 parallel mini rail tracks, hauled a full-size railway carriage nearly 33 feet at the DB-Gelände in Munich, Germany, on February 21, 2007. That's a mighty load for toy trains!

Here's a record to *CHOO CHOO* on! The **most powerful gas turbine-electric locomotive** is the Russian GT1-001, with a maximum capacity of 8,300 kilowatts (kw). The locomotive was tested in Shcherbinka, Russia, on January 23, 2009, and weighs some 600,000 pounds. It is designed for speeds up to 62 mph.

Here's a record to totally flip over. . . . High-end car manufacturer Jaguar organized the **largest loop-the-loop in a car** on September 14, 2015. At the wheel of the new Jaguar F-PACE, British stunt driver Terry Grant circled inside a loop with an overall diameter of 62 feet, 7.1 inches.

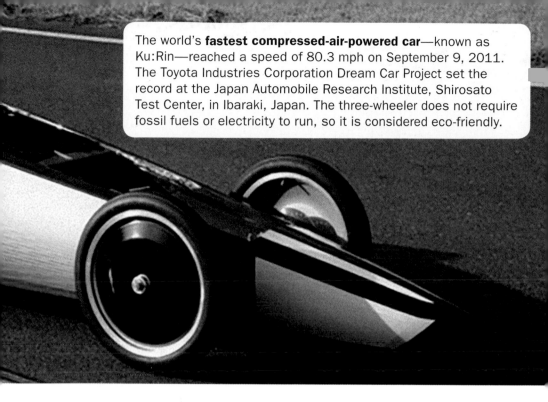

The world's **fastest compressed-air-powered car**—known as Ku:Rin—reached a speed of 80.3 mph on September 9, 2011. The Toyota Industries Corporation Dream Car Project set the record at the Japan Automobile Research Institute, Shirosato Test Center, in Ibaraki, Japan. The three-wheeler does not require fossil fuels or electricity to run, so it is considered eco-friendly.

The **fastest steam-powered car**, named Inspiration and designed by the British Steam Car Team, reached a steamy 139.84 mph on August 25, 2009. American investor Charles Burnett III drove the vapor vehicle at Edwards Air Force Base in California.

This record-breaker is electrifying! On April 17, 2012, Croatian engineer Mate Rimac drove the **fastest quarter mile by an electric car**. He achieved the feat in 11.85 seconds in a modified BMW M3 E30, at ETC, in Velika Gorica, Croatia. As part of the same record attempt, Rimac also secured the **fastest eighth mile by an electric car**: 7.60 seconds.

On November 15, 2010, students and teachers of the Automobile Engineering Course of Okayama Sanyo High School in Asakuchi, Japan, achieved a Guinness World Records title, but they don't like to brag about it. In fact, they like to keep their record on the down *low*! They built the **lowest roadworthy car**, which stands just 17.79 inches off the ground at the highest part of the car. The vehicle is nicknamed Mirai, which means *future* in Japanese, but it could be called the world's *lowest* lowrider!

You've heard of a minivan, but how about a mini*car*? **The smallest roadworthy car** measures 25 inches high; 2 feet, 1.75 inches wide; and 4 feet, 1.75 inches long. Created by American custom carmaker Austin Coulson, the micromachine is licensed to drive on public roads at up to 25 mph and regularly features in military parades.

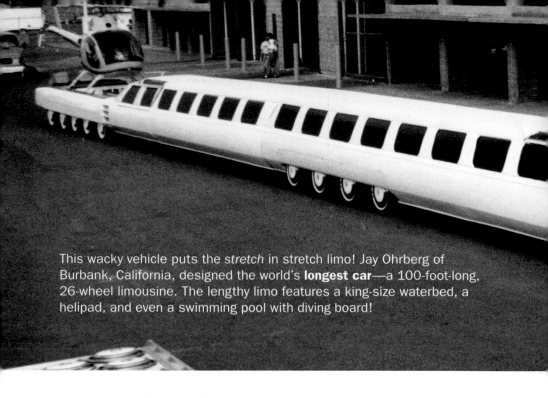

This wacky vehicle puts the *stretch* in stretch limo! Jay Ohrberg of Burbank, California, designed the world's **longest car**—a 100-foot-long, 26-wheel limousine. The lengthy limo features a king-size waterbed, a helipad, and even a swimming pool with diving board!

Americans Michael Machado and Pamela Bartholomew designed a unique limousine for people who want to live *large*—extra large! The 18-wheeled Midnight Rider measures 70 feet long and tips the scales at 50,560 pounds, easily making it the **heaviest limousine**. Inside there are three separate lounges and a bar, with enough room to fit 40 passengers.

Most limos are known for being super-long, but this one's a real *high* roller! The **tallest limo** measures 10 feet, 11 inches from the ground to the roof. Built by Australian husband and wife Gary and Shirley Duval, the extra-tall limo sits on eight monster-truck tires and has two engines.

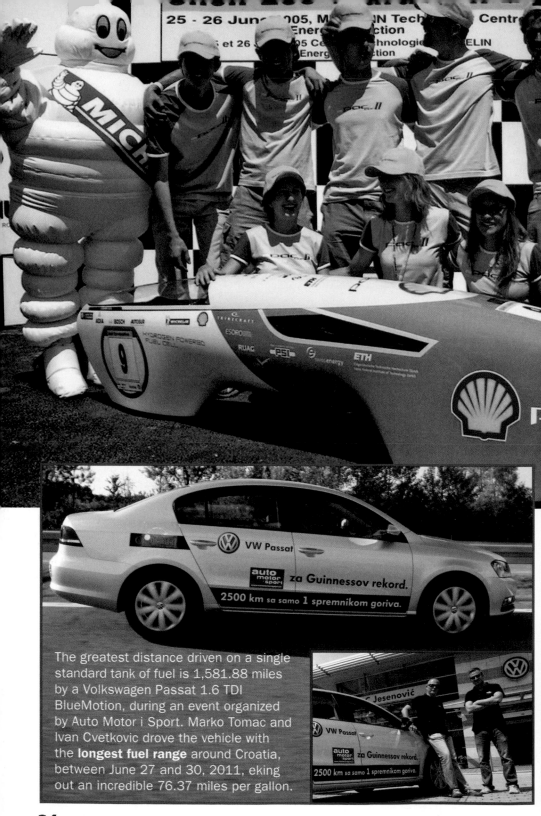

The greatest distance driven on a single standard tank of fuel is 1,581.88 miles by a Volkswagen Passat 1.6 TDI BlueMotion, during an event organized by Auto Motor i Sport. Marko Tomac and Ivan Cvetkovic drove the vehicle with the **longest fuel range** around Croatia, between June 27 and 30, 2011, eking out an incredible 76.37 miles per gallon.

Able to cover 15,212 miles for every gallon of gas, the PAC-Car II—made by the Swiss Federal Institute of Technology in Zurich—is the **most fuel-efficient vehicle**. It proved its green credentials at the Shell Eco Marathon at the Michelin Technology Centre in Ladoux, France, on June 26, 2005. The car has received a number of prizes for its innovation and fuel economy, including an Energy Globe Award and a Watt d'Or.

On May 29, 2008, at the High Speed Track of Nardò, Brindisi, Italy, the Mercedes-Benz Actros was recognized as the **most fuel-efficient 40-ton truck**—it achieved 6.88 gallons per 100 miles under test-drive conditions.

In 2003, this record-breaker just kept going . . . and going . . . and going. **The longest drive without recharging by a fuel-cell-powered vehicle** was undertaken by a modified Honda Insight car called MeVictory, made by InventQjaya. Powered by metal fuel cells, the vehicle traveled more than 325 miles in and around Kuala Lumpur, Malaysia, without refueling or recharging.

Simon Whitelock from the UK runs on all cylinders—and then some! He constructed the **vehicle engine with the most cylinders**, a motorcycle with a two-stroke engine that has 48 cylinders and a capacity of 256 cubic inches. The vehicle consists of 16 Kawasaki KH250 three-cylinder engines arranged in six banks of eight and is completely road legal.

This record-breaker should be nicknamed the *express*-o! On February 19, 2013, in Stockport, UK, Martin Bacon drove the **fastest coffee-powered vehicle**—it reached 65.536 mph. Talk about coffee on the go. . . .

Luckily, rocket sleds travel on tracks not ice, because this lightning-fast sled would melt anything in its path! The record for the **fastest rocket sled** was achieved at Holloman High Speed Test Track in New Mexico on April 30, 2003. The four-stage rocket sled system blasted to a speed of 9,468 feet per second in 6.031 seconds—the equivalent of 6,453 mph.

The ContiSportContact 2 Vmax is the **fastest road legal tire**, approved for speeds up to 223 mph, as verified in Munich, Germany, in 2006.

Building on two previous processions, the **largest fire truck parade** took place in Atoka, Oklahoma, on January 20, 2012, and comprised a total of 220 vehicles.

By land or by sea? Amphibious vehicles are adept at both. But on July 1, 2008, German Professor Hans Georg Näder and English Captain Henry Hawkins opted for sea only when they achieved the **fastest crossing of the English Channel by amphibious vehicle**: 1 hour, 14 minutes, and 20 seconds. They drove their land-and-sea vehicle, the *Tonic*, between Dover, UK, and Calais, France.

The world's **fastest fire truck** is *blazingly* fast! The jet-powered Hawaiian Eagle, owned by Shannen Seydel of Navarre, Florida, rocketed 407 mph in Ontario, Canada, on July 11, 1998. The truck is a red 1940 Ford powered by two Rolls-Royce Bristol Viper engines, which generate 12,000 pounds of thrust.

Bigfoot 5 is the monster of all *monster* trucks! This mega-size vehicle boasts the record for the **largest monster truck**, standing 15 feet, 6 inches tall; weighing 38,000 pounds; and sporting 10-foot-tall tires. It is one of a fleet of 17 Bigfoot trucks created by Bob Chandler of St. Louis, Missouri. Built in the summer of 1986, Bigfoot 5 is permanently parked in St. Louis, making occasional exhibition appearances at local shows.

KEEP ON TRUCKING

This monster truck is scary fast! On December 15, 2014, at the Circuit of the Americas in Austin, Texas, Mark Hall achieved the **fastest speed by a monster truck** while driving his Ram truck–sponsored vehicle, Raminator–hitting 99.1 mph.

On July 10, 2014, at Last Stop in White Hills, Arizona, American Russ Mann received the title for the **longest monster truck**: 32 feet.

The **largest land vehicle** is the 31.3-million-pound RB293 bucket wheel excavator. Manufactured by MAN TAKRAF of Leipzig, Germany, this earthmoving machine is 722 feet long, 310 feet tall, and is capable of shifting 8.475 million cubic feet of earth per day. That's the equivalent of more than 96 Olympic-size swimming pools every day.

Also in Germany, the Institut für Mikrotechnik Mainz and MicroToys e.V. EXPO collaborated to develop the **smallest forklift truck**. The little lifter measures 1.31 inches in length, 0.94 inches in height, and 0.64 inches in width. Perfect for delivering sugar cubes across your dining table!

This record-breaker puts the "motor" in "motorhome." Driven by Simon Robins of the UK, the **fastest motorhome** reached 141.3 mph at Elvington Airfield in East Yorkshire, UK, on October 21, 2014.

Talk about traveling light. . . . The world's **smallest caravan** is the QTvan. The cozy camper measures 7 feet, 10.9 inches long; 5 feet high; and 2 feet, 7.9 inches wide, but still packs in a single bed, a TV, and even a sink! Built by the British Environmental Transport Association, the QTvan was officially measured in Aylesbury, UK, on June 5, 2013. It's light enough that it can be towed by a bicycle!

Most golfers try to achieve a longer drive, but this drive really goes the distance! Mike's Golf Carts of Perry, Georgia, designed the **longest golf cart**, as measured on May 30, 2013. The colossal cart stretches 31 feet, 6.74 inches from bumper to bumper.

The world's **fastest golf cart**, meanwhile, is the Bandit made by Plum Quick Motors of South Carolina, which achieved 118.76 mph when driven by American Robby Steen at the Darlington Dragway in Hartsville, South Carolina, on October 31, 2014.

Take this cart on your next shopping spree and you'll be done in no time! The **fastest motorized shopping cart** hit 70.4 mph on August 18, 2013, driven by Brit Matt McKeown at Elvington Airfield in East Yorkshire, UK.

On the topic of record-breaking shopping carts, the **largest motorized shopping cart** measures 27 feet long, 15 feet tall, and 8 feet wide. It was constructed by Frederick Reifsteck and was displayed in South Wales, New York, on April 20, 2012. It's hard to imagine the bill at the check-out if you filled up this cart with shopping!

Talk about *rush* hour! The world's **fastest office** is a roadworthy desk, which travels at a max speed of 87 mph. On November 9, 2006, driver Edd China from the UK demonstrated the driving power of the high-speed office in London, UK, as part of Guinness World Records Day.

After weeding out the competition, Edd China achieved another title for the **fastest garden shed**. The high-octane hut, nicknamed Gone to Speed, hit more than 58 mph on the set of *Lo Show dei Record*, in Milan, Italy, on April 1, 2011. And this was no April Fools!

Talk about falling *fast* asleep! On November 7, 2008, in London, UK, Edd China also rode the **fastest mobile bed**—hitting 69 mph!

This vehicle doesn't stop for potty breaks; it breaks world records! On March 10, 2011, on the set of *Lo Show dei Record*, in Milan, Italy, Bog Standard achieved the record for the **fastest toilet**. This motorcycle and sidecar—hidden under a bathroom set—consists of bathtub, sink, and laundry bin, which can hit speeds of 42.25 mph. Once again, it was ridden by Edd China.

Whoa, baby! On October 14, 2012, at Shakespeare County Raceway in Stratford-upon-Avon, UK, Colin Furze drove the **fastest motorized baby stroller**. The speedy stroller achieved a top speed of 53.46 mph.

Why go to the chapel, when the chapel can come to you? The **fastest wedding chapel**—known as the Best Man—achieved 62 mph in Shelbyville, Illinois, on September 30, 2010. Despite its diminutive dimensions, the mobile church has stained-glass windows, a pulpit, pews, and even a pipe organ!

This go-kart can really *go*! In fact, on September 23, 2015, Tim Dellendorf set a new record time for the **fastest 0 to 60 mph acceleration by an electric kart**: 2.635 seconds! The vehicle was a collaborative project between Hochschule Osnabrück Institut MuT, WITTENSTEIN Cyber Motor GmbH (both of Germany), and H-Tech AG of Liechtenstein.

Talk about going to the X-treme! Pro skateboarder Rob Dyrdek and Joe Ciaglia (pictured left) built the **largest skateboard**, which measured 36 feet, 7 inches long; 8 feet, 8 inches wide; and 3 feet, 7.5 inches high. They unveiled the board on February 25, 2009, on the MTV series *Rob Dyrdek's Fantasy Factory*. That's one gnarly ride!

This lawn mower moves at a pretty good *clip*. Built and driven by Per-Kristian Lundefaret of Norway, the modified Viking T6 reached a blistering 133.57 mph on November 5, 2015, easily making it the **fastest mower**. Just think how much time this could shave off your lawn-mowing chores!

In January 2006, Hammacher Schlemmer & Company, Inc. released the **fastest hover scooter**. The Levitating Hover Scooter floats a few inches above the ground and has a top speed of 15 mph. The 1.3-gallon engine will provide up to one hour of futuristic fun!

LONG-DISTANCE LAWN MOWER

American Gary Hatter holds the record for the **longest journey by a lawn mower**. He traveled more than 14,500 miles in 260 days, setting out from Portland, Maine, on May 31, 2000, and arriving in Daytona Beach, Florida, on February 14, 2001.

Developed by Sony's Michihiro Hino in Tokyo, Japan, in 2002, the **smallest radio-controlled (RC) car** is 0.039 inches long. The model is a perfect 1:90-scale reproduction of a Mercedes-Benz smart car. It must be easy to park in tight spaces!

The **smallest RC model sailing boat** is 3.86 inches long, 1.81 inches wide, and 11.22 inches high. It was built by Italian Pasquale De Vito, and tested on June 10, 2014. It even features a working boom and rudder, just like its full-size counterparts.

Guinness World Records don't all *require* batteries, but for this record they are included—thanks to David Stevens. On April 20, 2013, at the Templestowe Flat Track Racing Club in Victoria, Australia, he achieved the **longest distance by a battery-operated RC model car**—23.79 miles! The 1:10-scale Formula 1 car went the distance on a single charge.

On June 22 to 23, 1997, at the Domaine Provincial of Chevetogne, Belgium, Laszlo Begovics and Reginald Tripnaux took turns at the controls to set the **longest distance by a battery-powered model boat in 24 hours**. They piloted the 31-inch scale model boat continuously on one battery over a distance of 52.97 miles. Wouldn't you like to see that in your neighborhood park's pond?

This record literally came down to the wire! The **longest cable car beneath sea level** connects Elisha's Spring with the Mount of Temptation in Jericho, Palestine. The 12-cabin cable car is 4,359 feet long, and the upper station is 165 feet below sea level.

The Ba Na Cable Car near Da Nang City, Vietnam, boasts the **highest nonstop single-track cable car**—reaching 4,488 feet. It opened to the public on March 29, 2013.

The **longest nonstop double-track cable car** is the Tatev Aerial Tramway, which covers a distance of 18,871 feet in Armenia, as verified on October 16, 2010. With the journey lasting about 11 minutes, the car connects the village of Halizor with the medieval Tatev Monastery, passing over the Vorotan River Gorge, in places 1,180 feet below.

The Dubai Metro in UAE is the **longest driverless metro network**, with two lines totaling 46.41 miles. It was constructed by the Roads and Transport Authority, and officially opened on September 9, 2011. The system also holds the record for **longest driverless metro line**: 32.37 miles.

The **largest front-end loader** is the LeTourneau L-2350. This massive earthmover can lift 578,000 pounds in its 53-cubic-yard capacity bucket. A giant 2,300-horsepower engine drives the massive vehicle.

The Chiba Urban Monorail near Tokyo, Japan, boasts the **longest suspended monorail network** in the world—9.45 miles. The first 1.99-mile stretch opened on March 20, 1979, and the line has been expanded three times since. Roughly 120 trains run on the system each day.

Developed to test the integration of several miniaturized components, the **smallest motorized excavator** is a mere 2.48 inches long and weighs 0.42 ounces. It was manufactured by the Institut für Mikrotechnik in Mainz, Germany, in May 1998. The boom was made from brass, and the unit was powered by two micromotors, each 0.196 inches long. Just don't expect to use this on a big dig.

The **largest square-rigger** in service is the *Royal Clipper*. The massive ship is 439 feet in length with 56,000 square feet of canvas on five masts. It has 42 sails reaching 197 feet above the waterline, which propel the vessel to speeds of 20 knots. Used as a cruise ship, the *Royal Clipper* can carry 228 passengers and a crew of 106.

Imtech

Some world records are achieved the hard way—or sideways, at least! The *MV Hunte Stern*, a 610-foot-long chemical tanker built by Nanjing Jinling Shipyard in China, is the **largest vessel ever launched sideways**. On its introduction to the water in 2003—which took a painstaking 9.5 hours—the vessel weighed 22 million pounds.

Mont (previously called *Seawise Giant*, although it had other names prior to that) was the **largest ship ever built**, so when it was decommissioned in 2010, it also became the **largest ship ever scrapped**. The ultralarge crude carrier had a deadweight of 1,243,407 pounds and was in excess of 1,502 feet long—that's more than the combined lengths of four football fields.

SHIP, SHIP HOORAY

The **largest aircraft carrier cruiser** is the Russian Navy's *Admiral Kuznetsov*, commissioned in 1990. The ship measures 991 feet, 9.5 inches long with a beam of 237 feet, 2.4 inches.

In 1968, the Iowa-class USS *New Jersey* achieved a top speed of 35.2 knots, the **fastest speed by a battleship**. Powered by eight fuel oil boilers and four propellers, the battleship sustained the record-breaking speed for six hours.

American Robert Torline knows how to catch the breeze! He completed the **longest wind-powered journey on land** between April 29 and June 16, 2001, traveling from Brownville, Texas, to Maida, North Dakota, and covering a distance of 2,119 miles on his street sailer. The vehicle is essentially a huge skateboard with pneumatic wheels, powered by a windsurfer sail.

SECTION THREE

ELECTRONIC & CONSUMER GOODS

A s well as huge things like buildings, bridges, and ships, engineers and designers are just as important in the manufacture of everyday items, such as phones, computers, toys, and even clothes. In this section, discover ordinary electronics and consumer goods that became extraordinary record-breakers—from the largest television to the smallest book to the longest swing.

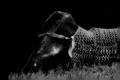

The **largest television** ever made was the Sony Jumbotron color TV screen, built for the Tsukuba International Exposition '85 near Tokyo, Japan, in March 1985. It measured a cinematic 80 feet by 150 feet.

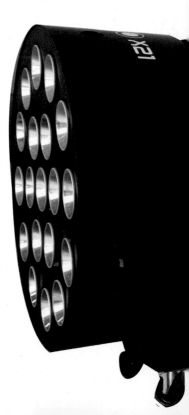

When it comes to this next record, it's lights-out for the competition! Made by Consolidated Edison, Inc., the world's **largest working light switch** had a plate measuring 40 feet tall by 24 feet wide, and a mechanical toggle base approximately 8 feet in height. The supersize switch was installed on the Broadway-facing facade of the Marriott Marquis hotel in Times Square, New York City.

At a dance party, you'd expect to have a ball—but maybe not one this big! On September 7, 2014, music festival Bestival, held at Robin Hill Country Park, on the Isle of Wight, UK, displayed the **largest disco ball**: it was a dazzling 33 feet, 10 inches in diameter. The owner of the company who made the giant glitter ball said, "It's taken the team three months of blood, sweat, and mirror tiles to fabricate this beast—it's been a fantastic journey."

The **largest flashlight** measures 13 feet, 1 inch long and 3 feet, 1 inch in diameter, and was created in 230 hours by Zweibrüder Optoelectronics GmbH & Co. KG of Germany. It consists of 19 LEDs, which is comparable to 250 light bulbs.

If engineering were a sport, this next record-breaker would be a league leader! On February 11, 2014, at the Texas Motor Speedway in Fort Worth, Texas, Panasonic set up the **largest high-definition television screen at a sporting venue**. The display measured 94 feet, 6 inches by 218 feet, 4.8 inches, making a vast viewing area of 20,614.31 square feet.

With only three units made, the PrestigeHD Supreme Rose TV is the **most expensive television** ever sold. Made from 61 pounds of 18-karat rose gold, and inset with 72 brilliant 1-carat flawless diamonds, the TV costs an unbelievable $2,250,000. With all that "bling," you'd probably feel very regal watching TV on this set!

Pump up the volume! The **loudest motorcycle audio system** produces a sound-pressure level of 143 decibels—about the same as a jet engine from 100 feet away. Denis Podshivalov of Russia showcased his ear-popping ride at an International Auto Sound Challenge Association competition in Omsk, Russia, on July 28, 2012.

Pump up the water! In 2004, Nijhuis Pompen of Winterswijk in the Netherlands created the **most powerful water pump**. The machine can get through 15,850 gallons per second, which means theoretically it could empty an Olympic-size swimming pool in about 42 seconds!

This next world record is a real *gas*! The **largest functioning gas turbine** is 43 feet, 5 inches long; 19 feet, 5 inches wide; and 16 feet, 4 inches high. Siemens AG Energy Sector built the turbine in Berlin, Germany, in 2007. Thanks to its innovative design, the engine requires a lot less fossil fuel than many smaller models, making it more efficient.

The world's **smallest electric motor** measures a tiny one nanometer across and consists of a single molecule of butyl methyl sulfide on a copper surface. The molecule spins under the influence of an electric charge introduced by the tip of a microscope. Scientists at the Department of Chemistry at Tufts University, in Massachusetts, achieved this feat in September 2011.

If you're looking for a sign, look no further! In 2013, Nissan Motor Co., Ltd built the **largest indoor illuminated sign**, spanning more than 1,874 square feet, at Dubai International Airport in UAE.

This next record was only a matter of *time*! The **smallest watch movement** belongs to the Cal. G720, developed by Citizen Watch Co., Ltd. of Japan in 2002. The tiny timepiece measures 0.046 square inches in surface area.

By contrast, American Jim Bowers created the **largest timepiece**: a clock with a face area of 3.25 square miles. The clock used lasers for its hands, each of which was a mile long. It was measured at the Burning Man festival in the Black Rock Desert, Nevada, on September 5, 2011.

The **largest rolling ball clock** is AION, which is 38 feet high; 19 feet, 8 inches wide; and 1 foot, 7 inches deep. It is located at the headquarters of watch and jewelry maker Bucherer AG in Lucerne, Switzerland, and was measured on March 11, 2008. A rolling ball clock displays the time by means of a series of balls and rails.

Sanwa Conveyor Co., Ltd. constructed the **largest globe clock** at Maruyama Park in Kasai City, Japan, in January 1998. Measuring 16 feet in diameter, the timekeeping orb weighs a mighty 8.8 tons.

This robotic dragon has a *step* up on the competition! The **largest walking robot** measures 51 feet, 6 inches in length; 40 feet, 5 inches in width; and 26 feet, 10 inches in height. On September 27, 2012, Zollner Elektronik AG let their monster loose in Zandt, Germany. The magnificent machine even breathes fire!

Why did the robot stay so busy? Because he was *wired*! That's certainly true for the Programmable Universal Machine for Assembly, more commonly known as PUMA. It holds the record for the **most widely used industrial robot**. The "bot" was designed by Vic Scheinman in the 1970s and manufactured by Swiss company Stäubli Unimation. This robot primarily does its heavy lifting in university laboratories and on factory assembly lines.

The **smallest humanoid robot** is the BeRobot, which measures 6 inches high and is able to walk, kick, and perform push-ups. The itty-bitty android was manufactured by GeStream and demonstrated at the Global SME's convention on September 6, 2007, in Kuala Lumpur, Malaysia.

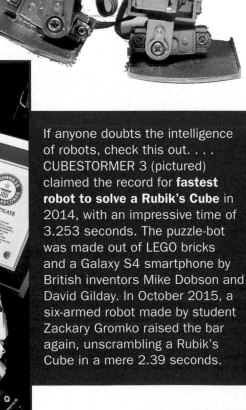

If anyone doubts the intelligence of robots, check this out. . . . CUBESTORMER 3 (pictured) claimed the record for **fastest robot to solve a Rubik's Cube** in 2014, with an impressive time of 3.253 seconds. The puzzle-bot was made out of LEGO bricks and a Galaxy S4 smartphone by British inventors Mike Dobson and David Gilday. In October 2015, a six-armed robot made by student Zackary Gromko raised the bar again, unscrambling a Rubik's Cube in a mere 2.39 seconds.

How do you fix a robot in space? With astro*nuts* and bolts! The **highest altitude for a robot conversation** is more than 257 miles above Earth. Japanese bot, Kirobo, achieved the feat on board the International Space Station with astronaut Koichi Wakata on December 7, 2013. The pair discussed various topics, including simple greetings and the training Kirobo received in order to go to space.

BREAKOUT BOTS

In October 2006, scientists at the University of California demonstrated the **smallest robotic hand**, which measures just 0.039 inches wide. Using silicon fingers and molecular balloons for joints, the hand could be made to flex and grasp objects by inflating or deflating the balloon joints.

The **largest robotic telescope** is the Liverpool Telescope. Owned by the Astrophysics Research Institute of Liverpool John Moores University, it is located on La Palma, in the Canary Islands, and its main mirror has a diameter of 6 feet, 6 inches.

This engineering marvel is *doggone* impressive! RS-01 Robodog is the world's **largest robot dog**, at 32 by 26 by 64 inches. Manufactured by RoboScience, the dog bot proved strong enough to lift a five-year-old child, although it would probably rather lift a big bone!

How many robots does it take to form the **longest chain of robots**? Two hundred fifty-five, to be exact! On November 26, 2006, students of the Lingnan Dr. Chung Wing Kwong Memorial Secondary School assembled the four-legged robots in Hong Kong, China.

Riddle me this . . . who holds the record for **largest mechanical puzzle**? That title goes to Joe Pieczynski. His 3D mechanical puzzle, called Quest, stands 57 inches tall, is more than 52 inches in diameter, and weighs 506 pounds. Pieczynski unveiled the huge puzzle, comprised of 209 separate pieces, in Austin, Texas, in 1998.

Local knitting clubs must love this record holder—the **largest spinning wheel** is more than 13 feet tall and stands in a town square in Sainte-Germaine Boulé, Quebec, Canada. It was erected in 1983 to celebrate the 50th anniversary of the founding of the town. The wheel itself has a diameter of 8 feet, and the entire machine, which weighs some 880 pounds, is powered by electricity.

On March 18, 1997, David Levy, an ergonomics graduate at Massachusetts Institute of Technology, patented the **smallest computer keyboard**. With complete alphanumeric, symbol, and command keys, the record-breaking device has 64 keys and measures just 3 by 1.2 inches. Smaller than a credit card, you can operate it with just your thumb!

Here's one computer mouse that suits its diminutive name! The **smallest mouse** is the Cat Eye FinRing. It is worn on the finger, just like a ring, and has three buttons that are operated by the thumb. It is cordless with internal sensors, which allow the pointer to be moved around the screen by tilting the hand.

What does a baby computer call his father? Data! First used in April 1951, the Harwell Dekatron Computer (also known as WITCH—Wolverhampton Instrument for Teaching Computation from Harwell) could also be called the father of all computers. It is the **oldest working digital computer**. Currently located at the National Museum of Computing, in Bletchley Park, UK, the pioneering technology underwent a complete restoration from 2009 to 2012.

The **highest data transmission rate over hollow-core optical fiber** is 73.7 terabits per second (Tb/s), which was achieved by engineers from Coriant R&D GmbH in their tests as part of the MODE-GAP program. The results were published in the *Journal of Lightwave Technology* on February 15, 2014. Using this technology, slow internet speeds could become a thing of the past; for instance, it would allow about 10,000 full-HD movies to be downloaded in a fraction of a second!

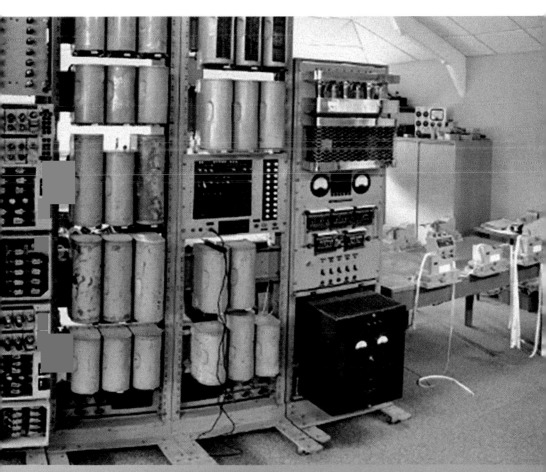

The world's **largest telephone** made its debut on September 16, 1988, at a festival to celebrate the 80th birthday of Centraal Beheer, an insurance company based in Apeldoorn, the Netherlands. It was 8 feet, 1 inch high and 19 feet, 11 inches long, and weighed more than 7,716 pounds. The handset, being over 23 feet long, had to be lifted by crane to make a call!

At last, a phone made *exclusively* for small talk! On September 16, 1996, Jan Piotr Krutewicz from Munster, Indiana, achieved the record for the **smallest telephone**. It measured just 1.87 inches by 0.39 inches by 0.82 inches.

When it comes to cell phones, bigger generally isn't better. But it is when it achieves a Guinness World Records title! The **largest cell phone** is a scaled-up Samsung SCH-R450, made by Cricket Communications and Samsung Mobile. It measured 15 feet by 11 feet, 2.4 inches by 2 feet, 6 inches at an event coordinated by the creative agency Neverstop in Chicago, Illinois, on March 11, 2009. Spectators were encouraged to send text messages and make calls from the phenomenal phone to their own devices.

MOBILE MILESTONES

Made of 18-karat gold and studded with more than 100 diamonds, the **most expensive mobile phone** was designed by GoldVish of Geneva, Switzerland, and was sold for $1,287,200 at the Millionaire Fair in Cannes, France, on September 2, 2006.

The **highest altitude text message** was successfully sent at 29,029 feet. Rod Baber from the UK achieved the feat using a Motorola MOTO Z8 on the summit of Mount Everest, Nepal, on May 21, 2007. His message read, "One small step for man, one giant step for mobilekind—thanks Motorola."

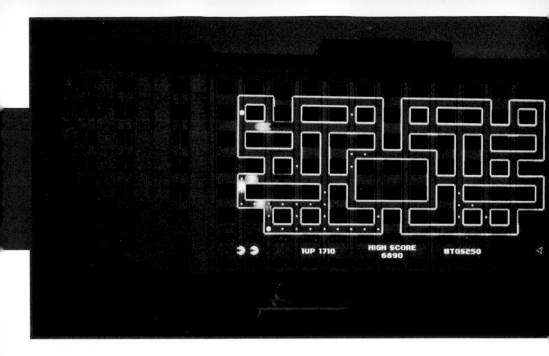

The **largest interactive whiteboard** could teach all other whiteboards a lesson . . . in record-breaking! Created by Osnes Nordic Group AS, the whiteboard measured 49 feet, 2 inches long and 3 feet, 11 inches high at the Skoleforum exhibition in Lillestrøm, Norway, on February 17, 2010.

On November 18, 2013, the UK television show *The Gadget Show,* achieved the **largest architectural projection-mapped game**. To secure the record, they projected a 23,881-square-foot version of Namco's *PAC-MAN* onto the Millennium Mills building at the ExCeL center in London, UK. Players controlled the gigantic game with an oversize joystick, located on the other side of the River Thames.

Ota City in Japan put on an illuminating spectacle on November 16, 2013, with a staggering 24,765 lights forming the **largest display of solar-powered LEDs**. Over a thousand more LEDs were included but had to be discounted because they went out during the attempt.

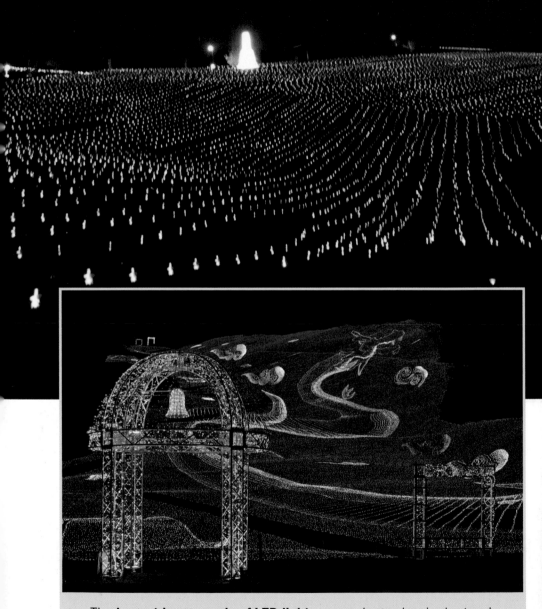

The **largest image made of LED lights** was a dragon-inspired artwork containing 1,529,103 lights and was created by Motoo Maruta at APA RESORT JOETSU-MYOKO, in Myoko, Japan, on June 28, 2015.

When life gives you lemons, make world records! The **most power drawn from a fruit battery** is 1.21 watts and was achieved by Da Vinci Media at the Campona Shopping Center in Budapest, Hungary, on April 27, 2013. Although the feat required 1,500 lemons, nobody was left with a bitter taste that day.

On July 7, 2012, in Erlangen, Germany, Marie-Therese Gymnasium achieved the record for the **highest voltage from a potato battery**—1,224 volts. That's definitely no small potatoes! In fact, that's nearly the same voltage output by 1,000 AAA batteries!

Electricity and water don't mix—but this record proved an exception!
On April 13, 2010, Australian Lloyd Matthew Godson generated the
most electrical energy by pedaling underwater—2,502.2 watt-hours.
Godson achieved the record at LEGOLAND Atlantis by Sea Life in
LEGOLAND Deutschland, in Günzburg, Germany.

Row, row, row your volt! On October 20 to 21, 2011, in Nottingham, UK, 124 volunteers at the University of Nottingham produced the **most electrical energy by indoor rowers in 24 hours**—12.4 kilowatt-hours—enough to power a 100-watt TV for more than five days!

Riding on 48 bikes, more than 1,500 students and staff of the Hong Kong Polytechnic University produced 31,399.31 watt-hours of energy from September 11 to 12, 2014—the **most electricity generated by pedaling on bicycles in 24 hours**. Promoting renewable energy and healthy living, the output was used to power 50 LED lights across the campus.

The sun is always shining on this record. The **most powerful building-integrated photovoltaic power station** (a building that converts sunlight into electricity) is owned by Shanghai Automotive Asset Management Co., Ltd. and has a total capacity of 20.013 megawatt peak (MWp). Even on overcast days, power is still generated. Located in Nanjing, China, the plant—positioned on the top of a multi-story car park—was completed in December 2013.

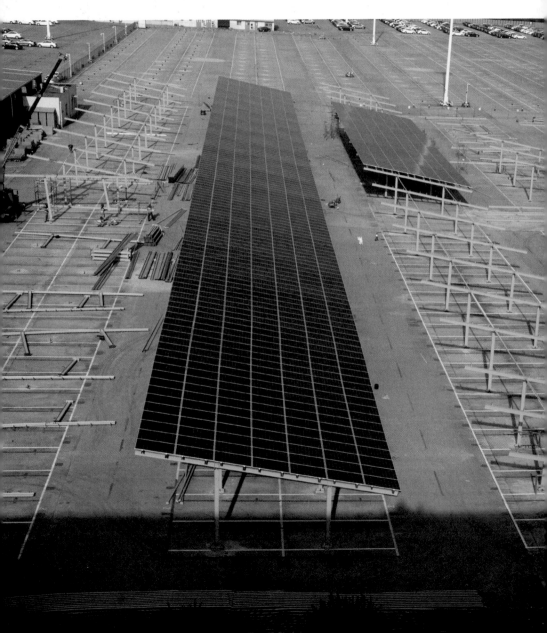

Talk about brainpower! The **heaviest machine moved using a brain-control interface (BCI)** weighed 61.95 tons, as demonstrated on the set of *The Gadget Show* in the UK, on March 17, 2011. The four presenters of the TV science series moved cranes using their brain waves in order to pick up and transport a car with an electromagnet. A BCI works by detecting the electrical signals that naturally occur in our brains, interpreting what they mean, and then translating these into mechanical instructions.

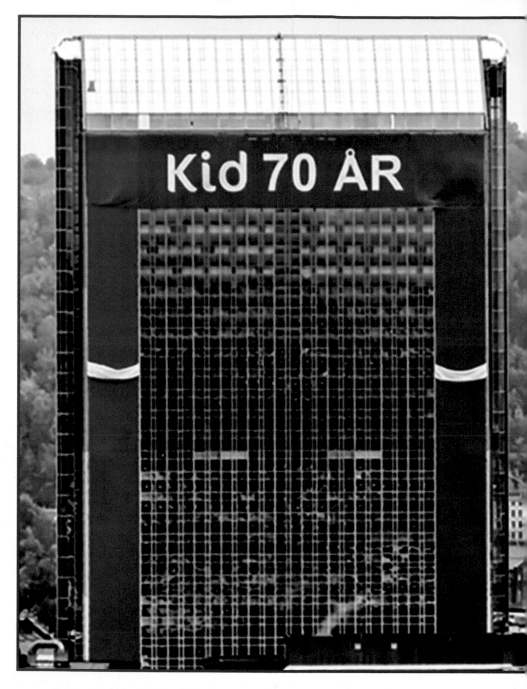

On October 3, 2008, Kid Interior Design brought the curtain down on the competition by unveiling the world's **tallest curtains** on the facade of the Radisson Blu Plaza Hotel in Oslo, Norway. Each drape measured more than 213 feet high, and took a team of 25 people a week to make.

Using an ultrathin layer of carbon fibre, Massimiliano Della Monaca designed the **lightest chair**, weighing a miniscule 1 pound, 5.7 ounces—about the same as an NBA basketball. The Estrema chair was presented in Marina di Carrara, Italy, on October 30, 2008.

On July 25, 2014, in Saratov, Russia, furniture maker Mnogo Mebeli manufactured the **longest sofa**. It measured more than 3,302 feet and is estimated to seat around 2,500 people. Your whole neighborhood could curl up on it!

On March 19, 2013, in Lake Charles, Louisiana, American Christopher Cruze achieved the record for the **longest bench swing**. It measures 59 feet, 11.6 inches, with the seating area spanning 59 feet, 2.6 inches—long enough to fit about 40 people.

On September 2, 1998, eight volunteers from the village of Havelte in the Netherlands constructed the world's **longest swing**. Built in two days, the wooden swing was 439 feet, 7 inches long and made from 132 poles and 4,921 feet of rope. The swing, which can accommodate 288 children at once, was made especially for the local community to enjoy.

The **largest tapestry** depicts famous historical figures, such as Winston Churchill and Albert Einstein, but it's a historic work in and of itself. In 1995, after five years in the making, Belarusian artist Alexander Kishchenko completed the *Tapestry of the Century*. The woven artwork stretches approximately 62 feet tall and 45 feet wide with a total area of 2,859 square feet.

Roll out the red carpet for this next Guinness World Records title holder! The **largest handwoven carpet** was a single piece that measured more than 10,957 square feet. Made by the Beijing Jin Bao Hua Carpet Manufacturing Co., Ltd. it was verified on August 28, 2013. This pales in comparison to the **largest multi-piece handwoven carpet** (pictured), manufactured by the Iran Carpet Company. This had a total area of 60,600.81 square feet, as confirmed in Abu Dhabi, UAE, in 2007.

Honk! Honk! The **loudest bicycle horn** is capable of producing a sound pressure level of 136.2 decibels— about as loud as a firecracker! The Hornster was developed by the Environmental Transport Association and demonstrated by Yannick Read on February 13, 2013, in Weybridge, UK.

Twelve times the size of its real-world inspiration, the **largest electric guitar** is 43 feet, 7.5 inches tall and 16 feet, 5.5 inches wide and weighs 2,000 pounds. Students from Conroe Independent School District Academy of Science and Technology in Texas modeled their creation on a 1967 Gibson Flying V. With construction beginning in October 1999, the instrument was finally played at the Cynthia Woods Mitchell Pavilion on June 6, 2000, with the opening chord of "A Hard Day's Night" by The Beatles.

This next guitar definitely puts the "rock" in rock 'n' roll! On March 15, 2015, Aaron Shum of Hong Kong, China, broke the record for the **most valuable guitar**. The seven-figure six-string guitar, encrusted with more than 400 carats' worth of diamonds, is valued at $15.5 million (HKD) or $2 million (USD).

This record-breaking piano is truly *grand*! Daniel Czapiewski of Poland constructed the world's **largest piano**, measuring 8 feet, 2 inches in width; 19 feet, 10 inches in length; and 6 feet, 3 inches in height. Czapiewski played the piano, which has 156 keys (68 more than a standard-size piano), at a concert in Szymbark, Poland, on December 30, 2010.

The Sri Veenavani Music School in Bangalore, India, gathered 400 students to play in the **largest keyboard ensemble** on September 6, 2015. The young musicians played a variety of songs during the mass performance, including the Indian national anthem.

154

The **largest accordion** is 8 feet, 3.5 inches tall; 6 feet, 2.75 inches wide; and 2 feet, 9.5 inches deep; and weighs approximately 440 pounds. The instrument, built by Giancarlo Francenella from Italy, bears the name Fisarmonica Gigante and was completed in 2001. Built on a 5:1 ratio from the original, the mega-instrument is made of wood (fir, cedar, mahogany, and walnut), metals (aluminum and steel), cardboard, cloth, and special varnishes.

Using eight different types of wood, Eduardo Baltazar Solorzano Árcia from Mexico created the **largest marimba**, an instrument similar to a xylophone. On April 22, 2009, in Ocosingo, Chiapas, Mexico, the instrument measured 3 feet, 3 inches high; 13 feet, 5 inches long; and 4 feet, 8 inches wide at the bass end.

On March 28, 2013, in Neroth, Germany, Dietmar Weides squeaked out one big victory. On that date, he set the record for the **largest mousetrap**, measuring 19 feet, 9 inches long; 9 feet, 10 inches wide; and 11.22 inches thick. You'd have to have a pretty *big* vermin problem to ever need this!

In February 2007, in Murcia, Spain, Salzillo Tea and Coffee constructed the world's **largest coffee press**. It stood 7 feet, 6 inches high and was 2 feet, 4 inches in diameter and was estimated by the company to hold around 10,000 cups of coffee, which were served to the crowds who came to watch the record attempt.

THE WORLD'S BIGGEST COFFEE MUG

What on earth could hold all that coffee? The **largest mug**, of course! The fiberglass vessel measures 20 feet high, with an outer diameter of 14 feet. Constructed by Paarnassus Events, and commissioned by Consolidated Coffee Ltd., it was unveiled on August 14, 1998, at Bangalore Palace, India. The monster mug took 24 people more than 9,500 hours to make and could hold close to 11,000 gallons of liquid.

Talk about walking tall! On November 10, 2014, in New York City, NBC *Today Show*'s Jill Martin and shoe designer Kenneth Cole created the **largest high-heeled shoe**, which stands 6 feet, 1 inch tall and is 6 feet, 5 inches long. The giant shoe was unveiled on the *Today Show* as part of Guinness World Records Day 2014.

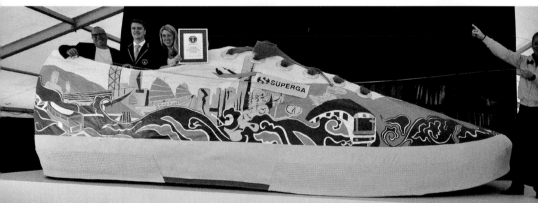

This epic footwear was always a *shoe*-in for the record! On April 12, 2013, in Hong Kong, China, Electric Sekki achieved the record for the **largest shoe**. The supersize sneaker—a replica of a Superga 2750—measured 20 feet, 11.97 inches by 7 feet, 10.09 inches and was 5 feet, 4.96 inches high.

These shoes certainly weren't made for walking, but they sure are a fantastic feat of carpentry. American craftsman Jim Bolin, from Casey, Illinois, earned the record for **largest wooden shoes** on October 20, 2015. Carved using a chainsaw, each clog measures 11 feet, 5 inches long and weighs about 1,500 pounds!

You shouldn't need to wear glasses to see this next record holder. The **largest pair of spectacles** were manufactured in December 2004 by Errold Jessurun, who works for opticians Jess Optiek, in the Netherlands. The specs are 6 feet, 4.25 inches wide, and each lens is 2 feet, 2.75 inches across. All the better to see you with. . . .

Construction workers wear high-visibility jackets so they can be easily seen for safety . . . and this one really can't be missed! The **largest high-visibility jacket** was 45 feet, 6 inches high and 35 feet wide. Created by Febelsafe and Secura, in Brussels, Belgium, it was measured on February 7, 2013.

Save this shirt for a *big* day! The **largest button-down shirt** was 214 feet, 6 inches long, with a chest of 172 feet, 11 inches and sleeves of 78 feet, 8 inches by 51 feet, 3 inches. It was made out of blue poplin and polyester yarn by clothes retailer Walbusch, and then laid out at the LTU-Arena, Düsseldorf, Germany, on June 25, 2009. The XXXXXXL shirt was made into 25,000 bags after the event, which were sold to raise money for the SOS Kinderdorf in Belarus.

衣物呵护

Even the most mundane of machines can become a record-breaker. For instance, a doll-size washing machine measuring 1 foot, 3 inches by 10 inches by 10.9 inches might not sound very practical, but it does make it the **smallest washing machine**. The tiny washer was made by Qingdao Haier Washing Machine Co., Ltd. in Qingdao City, China, and unveiled in 2011.

Manufactured by Neerja Roy Chowdhury of India, the **largest scissors** are a cut above the rest! They measure 7 feet, 7 inches from tip to handle, as verified on August 16, 2009.

The **smallest scissors**, meanwhile, belong to Chen Yu Pei of China. In August 2003, these scaled-down snippers measured 0.068 inches long and 0.054 inches wide. Chen is no stranger to the world of micro records; he also holds the title for **smallest teapot**.

It's "game over" for the competition with this record holder. The **largest arcade machine** was crowned in Bensenville, Illinois. Confirmed on March 23, 2014, the cabinet—made by Jason Camberis—measures more than 14 feet tall, 6 feet wide, and 3 feet deep. It can play a range of games, including the classic *PAC-MAN*.

The **largest 4K screen used in a video game competition** spanned 15,224 square feet and was powered by NVIDIA at Churchill Downs, in Louisville, Kentucky, on September 9, 2014. The players, Tom Lounsbury and Justin Munoz, used the supersize screen to compete in a *Borderlands: The Pre-Sequel!* competition.

Officially verified in August 2011 as the **largest console gamepad**, this fully functional Nintendo Entertainment System pad measures an enormous 12 feet by 5 feet, 3 inches by 1 foot, 8 inches—30 times the size of the original controller. Its main creator was engineering student Ben Allen, who was helped by Stephen van't Hof and Michel Verhulst, while studying at the Delft University of Technology in the Netherlands. The gamepad is so big that if you want to use it like a standard handheld controller, you will need to grow to 167 feet tall!

GET YOUR GAME ON

The world's **most successful coin-operated video game** is *PAC-MAN*. From its launch in 1981 until 1987, a total of 293,822 *PAC-MAN* machines were built and installed in arcade venues around the world. Designed by Tohru Iwatani of Namco in Japan, the original title spawned several sequels, including *MS. PAC-MAN* and *JR. PAC-MAN*.

Madden NFL (EA Tiburon) is the **longest-running sports video game series**. With a total of 30 games released in 26 years, the franchise is the frontrunner among all sports games as of June 2015.

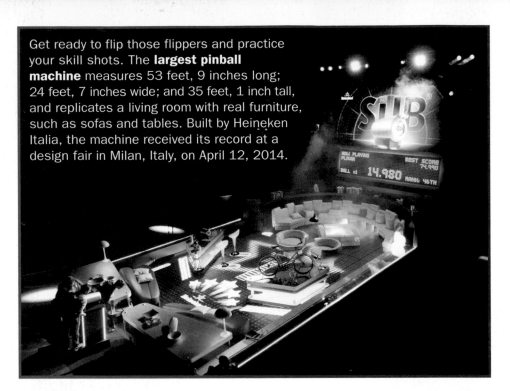

Get ready to flip those flippers and practice your skill shots. The **largest pinball machine** measures 53 feet, 9 inches long; 24 feet, 7 inches wide; and 35 feet, 1 inch tall, and replicates a living room with real furniture, such as sofas and tables. Built by Heineken Italia, the machine received its record at a design fair in Milan, Italy, on April 12, 2014.

At 17 by 8 by 12 feet, the epic Santa Claw holds the record for the **largest claw machine**. The device was operated via the internet between January and May 2011, with 100,000 players trying their luck at bagging a prize with the mechanical grabber. The Santa Claw has since made appearances at other major events, such as the 2013 Super Bowl.

The **largest capsule vending machine** measured 32 feet, 3 inches in height and 15 feet, 5 inches in width, and had a volume of 795 cubic feet. The Berjaya Times Square hotel and mall in Malaysia built the vast vending machine on July 20, 2013 to celebrate its 10th anniversary. Capsules inside contained coupons that could be redeemed for a range of prizes.

At the Tokyo Toy Fair in Japan, in May 2002, TOMY presented the **smallest sound-activated self-powered toys**. With a range of 10 different characters, its so-called MicroPets each measured no more than 1.37 inches tall and reacted to triggers such as clapping and people's voices.

In 2014, Sphere Corporation Limited of Hong Kong, China, brought out the **first wireless induction-powered aquatic toy**, a robo puffer fish called the LumiPUFF in its bowl. The best thing about this pet? It never needs feeding or to have its tank cleaned!

The **largest snowboard** shreds the competition! Manufactured by Arnold Schindler and his team from Schindler & Scheibling AG in Flumserberg, Switzerland, the behemoth board measured 32 feet, 9.7 inches long and 7 feet wide as verified on March 18, 2007. To prove it worked, 27 people rode the board simultaneously down a local ski slope.

Surf's up—*way* up! The Epic Big Board Ride and Visit Huntington Beach joined forces to create the world's **largest surfboard**, which stretches 42 feet, 1.5 inches long. On International Surfing Day— June 20, 2015—the Big Board was ridden simultaneously by 66 surfers off the coast of California, easily setting a new mark for **most people riding a surfboard**.

Japan Golf Equipment Co., Ltd. of Tokyo, Japan, knows a lot about exclusive clubs. They hold the Guinness World Records title for the **lightest golf club**! The driver, called the JBeam Win.1, weighs just 7.75 ounces, with just over two-thirds of its weight made up by the titanium head.

You might think that owning the **largest yo-yo** has its ups and downs, but setting this Guinness World Records title is definitely an up! The giant yo-yo is 11 feet, 10 inches across and tips the scales at 4,620 pounds. It was created by Beth Johnson in LaRue, Ohio, over three years and earned the record in 2012.

Going in circles doesn't always have to be a fruitless exercise. In fact, for TOSY Robotics JSC of Vietnam, it earned them a record. They set the **longest-running mechanical spinning top** in motion on May 23, 2011, after which it went on spinning for a dizzying 24 hours, 35 minutes, 15 seconds.

Hopefully there aren't too many sand castles nearby when this record holder is around. . . . The **largest beach ball**, created by Polish supermarket chain Real, is a staggering 51 feet, 10 inches in diameter. It bounced into the record books in Czluchow, Poland, on May 8, 2012.

Pop goes the world record! On April 19, 2013, almost 300 students and teachers in Taiwan worked together to achieve the record for **most pop-ups in a pop-up book**. The 3D scenes depicted local cultural hot spots, including temples and Taichung Harbor.

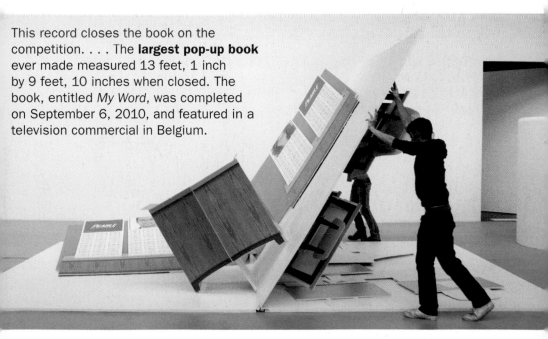

This record closes the book on the competition. . . . The **largest pop-up book** ever made measured 13 feet, 1 inch by 9 feet, 10 inches when closed. The book, entitled *My Word*, was completed on September 6, 2010, and featured in a television commercial in Belgium.

At the other end of the scale, the **smallest printed book**, titled *Flowers of the Four Seasons*, measures a microscopic 0.0291 by 0.0295 inches. Toppan Printing Co., Ltd. Printing Museum in Tokyo, Japan, published 250 copies of the 22-page book in 2012. The book is sold as a set, together with an enlarged version and a handy magnifying glass.

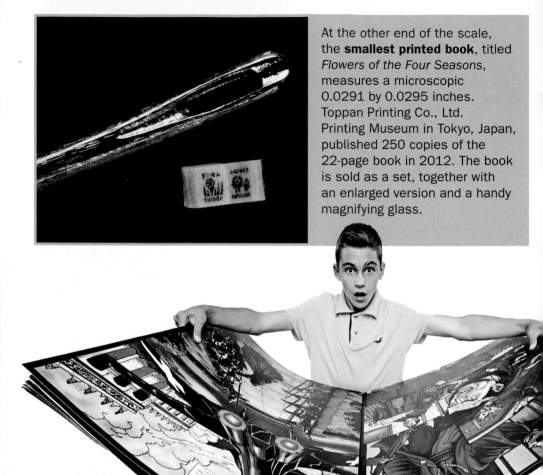

Bang! Wham! Blam! The **largest comic book published** is chapter one of the graphic novel *CruZader™: Agent of the Vatican*, by American comic writer Omar Morales. On August 30, 2014, the book measured 2 feet by 3 feet, 1.19 inches, as verified in Fremont, California.

BRING YOUR BIGGEST BOOK BAG

The **largest book** measures 16 feet, 4.8 inches by 26 feet, 5.2 inches. It weighs approximately 3,306 pounds and consists of 429 pages. Mshahed International Group unveiled their record-breaking book, titled *This Is Mohammad*, in Dubai, UAE, on February 27, 2012.

The **largest book pyramid** consisted of 63,377 books and was achieved by family-owned bookstore chain Ernster s.à.r.l. in Luxembourg City, Luxembourg, on April 28, 2015. The pyramid was constructed to celebrate the company's 125th anniversary.

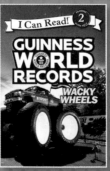